Hot Tracks
Careers in the Music Business

Julian Fleisher

SCHOLASTIC INC.

New York Toronto London Auckland Sydney
Mexico City New Delhi Hong Kong Buenos Aires

Illustrations
Marina Sagona

Copyright © 2002 by Scholastic Inc.
All rights reserved. Published by Scholastic Inc.
Printed in the U.S.A.

ISBN 0-439-12382-8
(meets NASTA specifications)

SCHOLASTIC, READ 180, and associated logos and designs are
trademarks and/or registered trademarks of Scholastic Inc.

LEXILE is a registered trademark of MetaMetrics, Inc.

4   5   6   7   8   9   10   23   12 11 10 09 08 07 06

Contents

Introduction

*Music is a world within itself, with a
language we all understand.
With an equal opportunity for all to sing,
dance, and clap their hands!*

That's what Stevie Wonder sings in his song "Sir Duke." That song is about the joyful power of music. Music can reach across borders. It can erase people's differences. Music can even make friends out of strangers.

Some people spend their lives making music. They do it because it's what they love. But it's also how they make their living. What a bonus!

Most of these people aren't singers or musicians. In fact, most of the work on any CD happens *behind the scenes.*

Mariah can break your heart with a love song. Ricky can really make you move. But behind every superstar there are lots of people you don't know. They make the business run.

They're not always looking to get famous. They just want to get music out to the fans.

So you might not be the next Christina, Shaggy, or Madonna. But you could be a great writer who creates hit songs. Or you might be the clever engineer who records the songs. Or perhaps you're good at business. You might become the head of a record company. These are all cool **careers** in the music biz.

In this book, you'll learn about different jobs in the music business. You'll hear from the people who do them. And who knows? Maybe one day you'll help create music that makes people sing and dance and come together.

Songwriter:
Lisa J. Cornelio

Lisa J. Cornelio is a songwriter. She lives in New York City and writes songs almost every day. Sometimes Lisa performs them herself. Sometimes other people sing them.

Songwriting is not an easy career. It takes patience to make it. You need to keep working at it. But Lisa wouldn't want any other job. Find out why.

Question: When did you start writing songs?
Answer: I started when I was a little kid in church. Then I got really serious about it in high school.

Q: What made you want to write songs?
A: I've always really enjoyed listening to other people's songs. So I started trying to write my own.

Q: That makes sense. Can you explain how you write a song?

A: First, I come up with the music on my guitar. I write what's called a **chord progression**. That's a short series of musical chords that repeats itself.

Then I build a **melody**. The melody is the music or tune that you sing. When I like that, I write the song's **lyrics** or words.

Q: What's the most important part of a song? The chords, the melody, or the lyrics?

A: For me, it's the melody. That's what people remember. But that's just my opinion! Other songwriters might disagree.

Q: What's your biggest challenge as a songwriter?

A: The biggest challenge is just doing it! It's hard not to stop halfway through. It's easy to tell yourself that the song is no good. Not giving up is by far the biggest challenge for me.

Q: Is it *that* hard to write a song?

A: Well, it's hard to write a *good* song. Sometimes, a great idea just pops into your mind. But turning that idea into a good song takes time and hard work.

Q: Say someone wants to write songs. How would they get started?

A: Start by learning to play other people's songs that you really like. Learn all you can about those songs. Learn what style they are written in. Learn how they are built. And think about *why* you like them. If you know why you like a song, you'll know how to write songs that you enjoy.

Q: Is that all? I have a feeling there's more to getting started than just that!

A: I think all songwriters should read as much as they can.

Q: What do you mean? Read books?

A: Of course! Read books, magazines, newspapers, poetry, and everything in between! It's really important to have as big a **vocabulary** as possible.

Q: Really? For songs?

A: Especially for songs! For example, you should know as many different words for "sad" as you can. The more ways you have of saying the same thing, the better your songs will be. And you should avoid using **clichés**. That's the biggest danger of all.

Q: What's a cliché?

A: A cliché is a **phrase** that's used too much. "Sweet as sugar" is an example.

Q: Why do you want to avoid clichés?

A: Because they keep songs from being fresh. People tune out when they hear an idea told the same way over and over again.

Q: Well, how many things are left in the world that haven't been said already?

A: Not many! But it's not *what* you say that matters. It's *how* you say it. That's what makes a songwriter great.

Q: Let's change the subject for a minute. Can I ask you how a songwriter makes money?

A: Of course! I make money mostly by selling my songs to other people. Then they sing and record them. I also get something called a **royalty**.

Q: Royalty? Is that from a king or queen?

A: Not quite! A royalty is a little bit of money that gets paid to the writer. She gets it each time a tune she wrote is played on the radio or TV.

Q: So, can songwriters make a lot of money?

A: You can if your song is a big hit. If it's not, you can't. But that's life. Making money isn't the main reason I write songs.

Q: What is the main reason?
A: It's what I love to do!

Q: So what's the best thing about being a songwriter for you?
A: Not having to go to the office in the morning! And getting chills when you finish a song you know is great.

Q: How do you know a song is great?
A: You know it in your gut. Or by the look on other people's faces when you sing it for them.

Q: Okay, so what's the worst thing about songwriting?
A: The worst thing is working other jobs to pay the bills while you try to write a hit song. At a regular job you get paid every week. But a songwriter can work for years before she can make a living. Still, it's worth it!

Q: Sounds like it. Do you enjoy listening to other people sing your songs?
A: Oh, yeah. It's a thrill! I can just sit back and enjoy my work. I also love when

somebody else brings new ideas to what I've written. They add their personality to my songs.

Q: Who is your favorite songwriter?
A: I like different writers for different reasons. I have a favorite person for words. I have another for melody. And so on. They change from day to day!

Q: Okay, one more question. Why does everyone like songs so much?
A: Songs tap into our hearts and brains all at once. And that's pretty incredible.

What's your favorite song? Why do you like it? What would you write about if you were a songwriter?

Lisa's Love Lyrics

Here's part of a song that Lisa wrote.

Lisa enjoys playing live shows and trying out her songs on audiences.

I'm Not Falling

When I saw you standing there
I knew I was about to be **ensnared**.
Such a smile, such precious eyes
They barely knew the meaning of
    what they **implied**.
Would they rescue me from my
    painted past?
Or **spark** desire sure to last?
What else was there for me to say?
Guess I could only deny feeling this way!

I'm not falling. I'm not, I'm not falling in love.

You're a beauty. I'm a fool.
Love is strange and lovers cruel.
That this is true can't be denied.
But still I find I'm trying to make you mine.
So rescue me from my painted past.
Spark desire sure to last.
What else was there for me to say?
Guess I could only deny feeling this way!

I'm not falling. I'm not, I'm not falling in love.

Recording Engineer: Paul Vazquez

Paul Vazquez is from New Jersey. He and his buddies grew up playing guitar and other instruments in garage bands.

*Today, Paul has one of the coolest jobs in the music business. He's a recording engineer. He works with writers, **producers**, singers, and musicians. He brings their music to life by recording it in a **studio**. His work combines art and science in a **unique** way. Let's find out how.*

Question: Hi, Paul. So what exactly does a recording engineer do?

Answer: I'm the guy in the studio who records the music. I set up the microphones. I get the musicians ready to play. I let them hear each other. Then I record their **tracks** on tape or on the computer.

Q: What's a track?

A: Songs are recorded in separate pieces called tracks. For example, the piano is a track. The guitar is a track. The voice is a track, and so on. The final product is a combination of all the different tracks.

Q: Do you record each track at separate times?

A: You can. Sometimes we record a band's tracks on one day. Then the next day we record the singer's track. Other times we record all the tracks together.

Q: What do you do with the tracks?

A: That's the fun part! Each track is like a piece of a puzzle. You can fit them together in different ways. And you get different sounds and results.

Q: How do you do that?

A: You can add or subtract tracks. You can change the volume or add **effects**. One little change can make a really big difference in the way a song sounds.

Q: Now I get it. So how did you get started?
A: I started out as a musician. I played guitar and piano in high school. I was in lots of bands. And when we wanted to record our music, I was the one who did it.

Q: How did you know what to do?
A: I didn't! I just pushed the record button on a regular old tape recorder.

Q: Is it really that easy?
A: Well, in high school it was. Then in college I learned that real studio recording is much more complex and interesting.

Q: How so?
A: It's all about quality. Listen to homemade recordings like the ones I made in high school. You can hear the songs, but they sound small and distant. And you can hear all sorts of noise mixed in with the music.

Q: Why is that?
A: It's because a regular tape recorder can't capture most of the sounds a band makes. We were recording in a garage or living

room. It was hard to keep out the noise that we didn't want to hear.

Q: You mean like the neighbor's TV?
A: Exactly! Or your kid brother yelling at your sister! But things are very different in a professional recording studio. Studios are built to block out noise. Also, you use really expensive recording equipment that captures a whole lot more sound.

Q: I see. So you went from a little, store-bought tape recorder to a professional studio.
A: Yes. I wanted my recordings to sound like the CDs I bought in a store. But there weren't a lot of people who knew how to do that. So I taught myself.

Q: That's amazing! How did you learn?
A: I read a lot of magazines and books that I found in the library.

Q: Can you learn a lot on your own?
A: Yes. There's a lot of information out there if you look for it. But there's nothing like hands-on experience.

Q: How does someone get experience?
A: Go to a studio. Ask if you can help.

Q: Really? Just like that?
A: Sure! Recording studios are busy places. They're often looking for young people who will trade work for experience. Many places hire these young people when jobs come up.

Q: Is that what you did?
A: Pretty much. I got an **internship**.

Q: What's that?
A: That's when you help out at a place where you might want to work. You usually don't get paid. But you can learn a lot.

Q: Great idea. How can someone find out more about getting an internship?
A: Ask a teacher, career counselor, or librarian to help you.

Q: Now tell us more about recording. What do you like best about your work?
A: I really enjoy working with the musicians and their music. It feels great to help them

sound their best. It's really about trust between them and me.

Q: Trust?

A: Yeah, trust! These days there are more and more ways to record music. You can make things sound just as the musicians played them. Or you can add all sorts of cool effects. The musicians have to trust that you'll create the best sound for them.

Q: It must be great to sit back and listen to what you created in the studio.

A: That's what it's all about. A piece may sound like just a three-minute song to someone else. But to me, it's about all the things I did to make it great. I may have made the guitar solo more intense. Maybe I improved the sound of a voice. Or perhaps I made the whole band sound bigger.

Q: Do you have to be a musician to be a recording engineer?

A: No. Sound recording is mostly a science. It's like chemistry or physics. There are lots of **technical** things you have to know. Still, it helps to understand and love music. That way, you can communicate better with the musicians.

Q: What's the hardest thing about being a recording engineer?
A: That's easy! The hours. Musicians don't like to get up early. Sometimes we'll work late into the night. By the time we're done, the sun is coming up.

Q: What's another challenge?
A: Some musicians think they can record a whole CD in a day or two. But it takes a lot longer than that to record all the tracks. Sometimes one track can take all night!

What would you like most about being a recording engineer? What kind of music would you want to record?

Mixing It Up

A mixing board is where all the tracks of a recording are mixed together. So, what is a track? It's one piece of the whole recording. For example, one track could be the guitar part. One track could be the keyboard part. One track could be the voice, and so on. Mix them all together, and you've got a CD!

On a mixing board, each track has its own channel. Here's a close-up of one channel. Mixing boards can have dozens of channels.

Here's a look at a channel.

These knobs can control the effects. Effects are added to most tracks to make them sound better. One example of an effect is an echo. Another is compression. Compression is like volume, but different. It doesn't make a sound louder. It makes it seem closer.

These knobs control the equalization, or EQ, of each track. EQ refers to the amount of high and low sounds in the track. You could make someone's voice sound deeper by adding low EQ.

The pan knob controls where the track will be heard. Should it be heard more in the left speaker or the right one? This makes it easier to hear the separate instruments and voices in the final song.

The fader controls the volume of each track. Slide a fader up, and the sound gets louder. Slide it down, and it gets softer. Move it all the way down, and you get silence. (Often, the volume is called the level.)

Photos courtesy of Mackie Designs, Inc.

Composer: Butch Stewart

Butch Stewart writes and produces music for radio, TV, and movies. He owns his own commercial music company in his hometown of Chicago.

Because Butch is the boss, he can do whatever he wants. He makes his own hours. He calls all the shots. Let's find out more about his career.

Question: Butch, what is commercial music?
Answer: Commercial music is the music you hear on TV commercials. But that's not all. At my company, we write commercial music for radio and records, too. We also write music for films, as well as TV **themes**.

Q: What's a TV theme?
A: A TV theme is the music that you hear at the beginning and end of a TV show. It can be a song with lyrics. Or it can just be music without words.

Q: Have you written any themes that we might know?

A: Well, I wrote the theme for Oprah Winfrey's show.

Q: The music that opens her TV show?

A: Yup. That's Oprah's theme. I wrote and produced it.

Q: Wow, that's very cool. And I bet it was fun, too.

A: Yes, it was. And now, every time you watch her show you'll know you're hearing my music.

Q: Will we ever hear that music anywhere else? Like for another show?

A: Nope. That's Oprah's theme music. It's only for her show.

Q: So, how does your business work?

A: Well, I have my own company. We have a recording studio. There are lots of **composers** and producers here. My whole family works here too. We write and produce music for our **clients**.

Q: Your family! That sounds fun.
A: It's wonderful. They always understand what I'm going through here at work. If I'm late for dinner, they're late for dinner too!

Q: So, how do you figure out what kind of music your clients want?
A: We really spend a lot of time with our clients. We talk with them about their work. We ask them to imagine what their music should sound like. And we try to understand how they want people to feel when they hear the music.

Q: That's a lot to figure out!
A: It is. But I enjoy helping people make their dreams come true. It's fun to play them the different ideas that I have. We combine their needs with our talent. Next thing you know, there's music!

Q: How did you get started working in commercial music?

A: I've always had a **passion** for music. In high school I was in bands, choirs, and plays. And I've been in a garage band since I was in the sixth grade!

Q: What instruments did you play in all those bands?

A: Keyboards and saxophone. I also sang.

Q: That's a lot!

A: I told you I had a passion for music! One day, my sister-in-law Kitty introduced me to a record producer. He liked some of the songs I had written. So he decided to put them on a record.

Q: That sounds like very good luck. How does a person meet a record producer if their sister-in-law doesn't already know one?

A: Really, all you need to do is ask.

Q: Whom do you ask?
A: Everyone you know! You never know who might be able to help. You could even ask someone to be a **mentor**.

Q: What is a mentor?
A: A mentor is a person with wisdom and experience. He or she shares that experience with a young person. Mentors can help in lots of ways. They can give you personal and career advice. Almost everyone could definitely use a mentor.

Q: How do you find a mentor?
A: There are lots of ways. Libraries have information about mentoring programs. A teacher or guidance counselor can also help you. And, as always, parents or older friends can be of help too. You never know. They could even become your mentors!

Q: It sounds like mentors are a great idea even if you're not interested in music.
A: Sure thing! Everyone can use this kind of help from time to time.

Q: Now, let's talk more about your career. What do you love the most about writing commercial music?

A: I love working with singers and musicians. And I really love the whole process of making music.

Q: Could you explain what you mean when you say "the whole process?"

A: Sure! By *process,* I mean all the steps that are needed to create a great piece of music. The process is the most important thing. The final result isn't nearly as interesting as how you get there.

Q: You mean you don't care whether the result is any good?

A: No, no! I care deeply. But the results will only be as good as the work you do along the way. Sometimes, a piece of music doesn't turn out great. But I'll still enjoy the process of making it. I'm happy either way.

Q: Still, I bet you're happier when the results are great.
A: Of course! But I mean it when I say that it's the work that really matters.

Q: That sounds like it's true of a lot of things, not just music.
A: It's true of everything in life!

Q: Can I ask you another quick question?
A: Sure. Go ahead.

Q: Is Oprah nice?
A: Yes, she's the best! And she really likes the music we wrote for her.

What kind of person would your ideal mentor need to be? What kind of help would you like to get from this person?

Mentoring
Programs

A mentor can be very helpful, even if you're not interested in music.

There are lots of places to look for a mentor. You can begin with your local library. You can try a place of worship. There are also many groups that can help you find the right mentor. Here are just a few.

Photo courtesy of Butch Stewart

Butch takes time to show some kids around his studio.

Big Brothers Big Sisters of America®

The Big Brothers Big Sisters of America matches kids from single-parent families with adult mentors. It is the oldest and largest mentoring program in the country. They have offices in all 50 states. Check your phone book for an office near you. **www.bbbsa.org**

Boys and Girls Clubs of America

The Boys and Girls Clubs of America have more than 25 programs for kids. The easiest way to find out what's going on in your area is to call 1-800-854-CLUB. Or search their website. Click on "Find a Club." **www.bgca.org**

The National Mentoring Partnership

The National Mentoring Partnership can help you find mentor programs in your area. Just call 1-888-432-6368. Or search their website. Click on "Find a Mentor." **www.mentoring.org**

YMCA of the USA

Some YMCAs offer mentor programs. To find the YMCA nearest you, look in your local phone book or call 1-888-333-YMCA. You can also search their website. Click on "Find Your YMCA." **www.ymca.net**

YWCA of the USA

The YWCA offers a variety of programs for women and girls. Some YWCAs offer mentor programs. To find the YWCA nearest you, look in your local phone book. Or click on "Local YWCAs" on their website. **www.ywca.org**

Singer: Polly Segal

Polly Segal is a singer from Los Angeles. She's also been an actor. And she's been a writer. But she's made singing her career. We caught up with Polly between concerts. We wanted to ask her about the life of a singer.

Question: Polly, thanks for talking with us.
Answer: It's a pleasure! Besides, I'm between **gigs** anyway.

Q: Between gigs? What's a gig?
A: It's a weird word. That's what people in the music business call a show or a concert.

Q: Got it. So what does it take to have a career as a singer? Is it enough to have a beautiful voice?
A: Well, sometimes you don't even need a beautiful voice. It's more important to have

a voice that people remember.

Q: Can you give me an example?
A: Sure! Take Macy Gray. She's been incredibly successful. But not everyone thinks her voice is beautiful.

Q: So how *did* she become so successful?
A: She's a brilliant musician. She has great ideas about songs. And she can get those ideas across in exciting ways. And her funny voice has made her singing all the greater.

Q: Okay, back to *you*. How have you built your singing career?
A: It hasn't been easy! I spend more time looking for work than I do singing.

Q: What do you mean?
A: Unless you're a star, you spend a lot of time on the phone.

Q: Who do you have to call?
A: Bands, clubs, studios, and musicians. Finding work and planning gigs takes time.

Q: What else helps your career?

A: I take voice lessons. I listen to lots of music. And I go to see other singers perform.

Q: Do you steal their ideas?

A: Of course not! But all artists learn their **craft** by watching other artists. It's one of the best things about making music. Sharing ideas and trading sounds is a great way to grow as a musician.

Q: Okay, so you have your voice. You have your musical ideas. You have your classes. Now what?

A: Well, the most important thing of all is the songs. You have to find lots of songs that you truly love to sing.

Q: Where do you find them?

A: Wow, that's a hard question! There are so many answers. You can find songs on the radio. Or on CDs and tapes. Some singers write their own songs. Others sing new songs by writers they love.

Q: Finding songs sounds like a lot of work!
A: It is! But I love it. It can be more fun than taking a vacation. If you love what you do, it doesn't feel like work!

Q: And you love to sing?
A: There's nothing else I would rather do.

Q: What do you love about it?
A: I love how free it makes me feel. When I'm singing I feel as if I'm flying. And I love to hear the reaction of the audience when I'm doing a good job.

Q: That must be a thrill!
A: I wouldn't trade *anything* for it. I'm a singer! It's the best thing in the world!

What are some things you love to do? How could you use these things to build a career?

Singer's Stuff

Do you think singing is just a matter of belting out the tunes? Well, that's just the beginning! Here's a list of things that Polly needs at each gig:

- a change of clothes, so she'll always look good
- folders of sheet music
- a microphone and cable
- music stands and lights
- speakers and speaker cable
- lists of the songs to sing
- phone numbers of all her musicians and technical people
- hot tea for her throat
- press materials to hand out to radio and newspaper people
- business cards

Polly sends flyers to her fans to promote her gigs.

POLLY AT THE STINGER

Photo by Brent Helsel

DJ: Anthony Velarde

DJ is short for disc jockey. And DJs spin records. They used to be known mainly for playing records on the radio. But these days, DJs are the stars at clubs and parties.

One of these DJs is Anthony Velarde. He lives and spins in New York City. Let's find out how he spends his days (and nights).

Question: Hi, Anthony. First, explain to me what DJs do.

Answer: We select and play records. We figure out what songs sound good together.

Some DJs scratch. That means they move the record back and forth on the **turntable**. Others add other sound effects or live instruments. Still, most DJs have the same goal. They want to make people dance!

43

Q: When did you first become interested in spinning records?

A: When I was about eight years old. I used to put together collections on cassettes. Later, I started collecting records. I liked anything I could dance to.

One day, I asked myself, "What can I do with all these records?" So I bought my first DJ turntables. Those are high-quality record players. Then I started playing at house parties. My friends were saying, "Hey, you're a good DJ. Why don't you try doing it professionally?"

Q: So what does it take to become a good DJ?

A: DJs must learn how to match beats. You want to make the beat of one song work with the beat of the next one. That way, people will keep dancing. You don't want them to feel a change in the rhythm. Otherwise, you'll have what DJs call a "train wreck" on the dance floor.

Q: What else does it take to become a DJ?

A: Lots of practice. After a while, you learn what songs work well with each other. You get a feel for it. Then you start putting sets together. A set is two or three hours of songs that sound good together.

Q: Do you plan every song? Or do you usually **improvise** during a set?

A: I practice a lot, especially with new records. I'll put together some **sequences** at home. A sequence is four or five songs that work well in a row. Later, during a set, I may use those sequences. It depends.

Q: How do you get your ideas for sets?

A: I'm often **inspired** by other DJs. But when I go into a record shop, I only buy records that I really love. I never buy a record just because I think it will work on a crowd. It wouldn't be my own sound then. A good DJ has an individual sound and style.

Q: How do you stay current on all the latest music?

A: I spend a lot of time in record stores. Also, I read a lot of record magazines. I try to find out what's new and what's hot.

Q: So, let's say you have a gig coming up. How do you get ready?

A: Well, DJs have to get people out to their shows. So a few days before the gig, I send out emails. I make a lot of phone calls. And I put up flyers and posters.

On the day of the gig, I get ready. I might need to take my own mixer and turntables. Then, I pack 80 to 90 records. That's enough for a four-hour set. Next, I get dressed up and head to the club.

Q: That's a lot of records to carry! Do your friends help out?

A: Well, it's hard to get help. I live on the fourth floor. And I don't have an elevator! But my friends like to meet me at the club and help out. They get in free. And they get to hang with the other DJs, too.

Q: That sounds fun. So, how many records do you own?

A: I've collected about 1,000 new dance records in the last two years. I also have around 4,000 CDs.

Q: Wow, how do DJs make money to buy all those records?

A: Lots of different ways. Some DJs work with rappers or bands. Others produce their own CDs. Most spin at clubs. Some even play at coffee shops and bookstores.

Weddings and private parties pay really well. But you have to play a wide range of music. And you might need your own sound system.

Q: What kind of music do you like to play ?

A: I spin mainly Techno and Trance music. Techno uses heavy beats. It just keeps pumping. Trance is more laid back. But at the same time, it grooves. I use them both to create a nice flow throughout the evening.

Q: What do you enjoy most about your job?
A: I like to see hundreds of people get into the same vibe. It's great when people have fun to the music I spin.

Q: What's your worst experience as a DJ?
A: Well, at a party one night, I was really into the music. My headphones were on loud. My eyes were closed. And I was dancing around in the DJ booth. I didn't realize the speakers had stopped working! The club was totally silent. I looked up and everyone was just watching me dance!

Q: Yikes! So, do you have any advice for someone who wants to become a DJ?
A: Yeah, cover only one ear with your headphones! Seriously, you have to be patient and practice.

Also, you should make friends with other DJs. Listen and watch, and you'll learn a lot. When you're ready, borrow or buy some equipment. You can find good stuff at garage sales and thrift stores. Some record shops sell used turntables, too.

Then start playing for your friends. It's a good way to get invited to all the fun parties!

Q: Thanks for the tips, Anthony. One final question. Do DJs have fans?

A: We all want to! You have more fun, and you make more money. And it's cool when people thank you for making them dance!

Anthony's Top-Ten Spins

1. "Manipulate" by Ben Sims
2. "Road to Rio" by Santos Rodriguez
3. "Shoreline" by Max Graham
4. "Breathe" by Art of Trance
5. "Metropolis" by Oliver Lieb
6. "Intensify" by Way Out West
7. "Wide-Eyed Angel" by Origin
8. "Together We Will Conquer" by Paul Van Dyk
9. "Train of Thought" by L.S.G.
10. "Mercury and Solace" by BT

Music Writer: Melissa Harris

Melissa Harris is a music writer. No, she doesn't write music. She writes about music. There are lots of magazines, newspapers, and websites about music. For good writers, there's almost always something to write about. There's also good money to be made!

Question: Melissa, why did you start writing about music?
Answer: Because I love it!

Q: So why not become a musician?
A: Believe me, I would have! But I don't have a lot of musical talent.

Q: So tell us how you became a writer.
A: I majored in English in college. I knew how to write. I had been a dancer and a DJ before. So, I loved music, and I understood it, too. I wanted a career that would matter

to me and to other people. Writing about music seemed like the best choice for me.

Q: Were you right?
A: Yes, I was. Now I spend all my time working with musicians, performers, and producers. I help their fans understand what they are up to. I learn about music. And I get seats at all sorts of great concerts!

Q: But you have to write about all that, too! So tell us about that.
A: A magazine or newspaper **editor** will call me. They'll have a story in mind. It could be about a band, a musician, or a concert. They'll tell me what the story is about. They'll give me names and phone numbers of people to **interview**. And they'll tell me how long the **article** should be.

Q: And do they say how much you'll get paid?
A: Definitely!

Q: How does that work?
A: It's pretty simple. Most newspapers and

magazines pay by the word. The going **rate** right now is about a dollar per word.

Q: So a 500-word article would pay $500?
A: Yes. Some big companies pay much more. Others less. But that's the life of a **freelancer**.

Q: What's a freelancer?
A: Freelancers are people who work for themselves. We don't get a regular paycheck from one company. We earn money from different places. We build our living one job at a time.

Q: Are all music writers freelancers?
A: No. Many big magazines, like *Rolling Stone*, *Vibe*, or *People*, have writers on staff. That's really good for a lot of people. But I like being on my own. At least for now.

Q: How did you find work when you started out in this career?
A: I called the magazines that I liked. I asked to speak to the editors.

Q: Really? That's all?

A: Yes! Then the editors asked me for samples of my writing. I sent them things I'd written for school newspapers. Later, they called and gave me a job when they saw a good story for me.

Q: Is that how it works today?
A: If you're new that's how it would work. It's different for me now. The companies I work for all know me. They think I am talented. So they call me all the time. Now I get to write stories based on my own ideas, too. But that comes with time.

Q: What's the best part of your job?
A: I love the whole process! I love everything about putting an article together. Let's say I'm writing about a new band. First, I get a copy of their CD. I listen to that a couple of times very carefully. I really want to get a sense of their music.

Q: What's next?
A: Then I meet them! I ask them about their music. I also want to know about them as

people. Where are they from? What bands do they like? What are their dreams? Then I go see them in a concert. That's my favorite part. They send me a few tickets so I can bring friends along. Then I write the story.

Q: What's that like?
A: First, I come up with what's called the angle. That's the big idea of the article. Then, I mix in details, quotes, and musical ideas to complete the article.

Q: How long does that take?
A: Usually about a day. It can take a lot longer, though. And the first **draft** is never very good. I don't hand that in. I always leave myself enough time to rewrite and make corrections.

Q: So then you're finished, right?
A: Wrong. My editors have to read and approve what I write!

Q: What if they don't approve it?
A: They send it back to me with comments. Then I have to fix it.

Q: That sounds like school!
A: It is—a little. But don't get me wrong! Editing is great! I love to rewrite. I look forward to improving my work. And my editors are all really nice. That makes it a pleasure to work hard.

Q: Do you see yourself writing about music for a long time?
A: Oh, yeah. I love it. It's steady work. It pays well. It's **flexible**. It keeps me close to the music I love. It gives me the chance to be heard. There's really nothing about music writing that I *don't* like.

Q: I'm feeling that! And thank you for explaining it all for us, Melissa.
A: The pleasure was mine. Now, write on!

What skills does a music writer need to do his or her job well? Think it over and make a list.

Music Reviewed

Melissa's work takes her backstage—and then back home to her computer. Here's one of Melissa's articles, fresh from her printer.

Squeeze Play
By Melissa Harris

The boys of Squeezebottle are keeping it real. They are full of passion. They are **motivated**. And they are young. (Don Speck is 17. Twins Eric and Matt Martin are both 16.)

This grunge-pop trio is from Tampa, Florida. Their music is down-to-earth. And they may be a great **alternative** to other acts from their hometown. (There are many superstars from Orlando. Britney Spears, *NSYNC, The Backstreet Boys, and LFO are all based in the area.)

"We never want to be super slick. We're not like those other bands," says Speck. He's the lead singer and guitarist. "I mean, they're not even real. They are just products."

"True," says drummer Eric Martin. "A big company puts them together just to make money."

"Music is so important," continues Speck.

"Songs shouldn't be written by businessmen. Those songs are just for selling soda and makeup. It's insulting."

Squeezebottle dresses in jeans, t-shirts, and no-name kicks. They seem ready to put their money where their mouths are. They wrote their own songs. And they produced their first CD with their own money. Today, most bands need a company to back them. But these guys say they will never show brand-names on their clothes or instruments. But can Squeezebottle still make it big?

"Well, we've got one thing that none of those other kids have," says Eric Martin. "We rock!"

Other Gigs

You've just read about a few careers in the music business. But there are lots of other great jobs in music. Here's a list of some of them.

Back-up singers

Before many of the big stars were stars, they sang back-up for other singers. It's a great way for new singers to break into the business. But it's not for everyone! Your ear for **harmony** has to be perfect. Your voice should blend with others. And you should be ready to back up the star.

Booking agents

Booking agents get musicians jobs at clubs, concert halls, and festivals. With popular bands, it's an easy job. With new bands, it can be a lot of work.

Accountants

The music business is huge. Billions of dollars are made and spent every year! Someone has to keep track of it all. Some accountants work for big record companies. Others work for small-time musicians. They know where all the money is.

Music publishers

A songwriter's music can't be played by anyone else without asking the publisher. Publishers sell and **license** songs to singers, movies, and television. Music is a big-money business. And most of the money is in publishing!

Record-store owners

Sure there are "mega" stores in every town. But it's the small independent stores that make the difference. In these stores, new bands can sell their work. And rare music can be found. Music lovers are very loyal to small stores. They like the music and service they get there.

Music coordinators for film and TV

Music is a big part of all movies and TV shows. And someone has to decide what music best fits each story. That's the job of music coordinators.

They have to have a wide knowledge of different kinds of music. They also have to be good at making deals. Finding great music for a scene isn't enough. They want to get it for a good price!

Record executives

Record executives are in charge of a company's **label**. They decide which performers the label will record. Think you know what people like to hear? Can you pick out a winning band? Don't mind turning musicians away? Well, get to work! But if you're weak at heart, find a different career!

Choreographers

Choreographers create dances— ballet, jazz, hip-hop, stepping, or anything! More and more people love to watch dance or to dance themselves. So choreographers are more important than ever!

Lawyers

Lawyers run the music industry. Every deal is written by lawyers. Their job is to know the law and to protect their clients from harm. They also make sure their clients get the money they deserve.

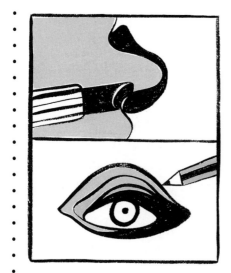

Makeup artists

Even beautiful people need help when the spotlight is on them. Makeup artists can be musicians' best friends. They help performers look great while they're performing.

Marketing managers

How do you sell a band or a musician to the public? That's what marketing managers figure out. They use magazines, radio stations, and TV shows to tell the public about their band. They also use T-shirts, posters, prizes, and other free stuff to grab people's attention.

Art directors

Most recordings have a look as well as a sound. Art directors make sure that a CD cover grabs your attention. If it looks cool, customers will want to pull it off the shelf.

Internet music distributors

These people use the Internet to sell music. It's a new business, and it's a huge one.

Musical arrangers

Creating a musical group's sound is the job of the musical arranger. Arrangers decide which instruments would sound best in a song. Sometimes they work with huge bands. And sometimes they work with musicians one at a time.

Record producers

They are in charge of the entire process of recording. They help everyone do their very best work. You may not see or hear them. But you can be sure they're there!

Publicists

Appearing on a talk show or on the cover of a magazine can make an artist's career. That's where publicists come in. They know the people who work at newspapers, magazines, and TV shows. They get on the phone and try to make their clients famous.

Artist's assistants

Musicians and other artists need lots of free time to work. That's why they often hire assistants to help them. Assistants usually work in a musician's home. So, they definitely have to be honest and friendly.

Music software developers

These days, most music is **digital**. It gets recorded directly into a computer. Engineers are always looking for new computer software for recording, editing, and mixing.

Instrumentalists

Instrumentalists are the most important people in the music business. They play the guitar, piano, trumpet, drums, saxophone, harmonica, or synthesizer. The list is almost endless!

Concert promoters

Bands love to play live on stage. Concert promoters make sure there's someone there to hear them! Their job is to get the word out. They do this through newspapers, magazines, and radio stations.

Bandleaders/Conductors

Some jazz and classical bands can get pretty big. These big bands need someone to guide them. Good bandleaders or conductors must be excellent musicians. They must be great at reading music. And they must be able to direct lots of musicians at once. Few people get as much respect as bandleaders and conductors do. And few people deserve it more!

Stylists

Who makes all those stars look so good? Who chooses all their cool clothes? Their stylists, that's who. Do you love fashion, beauty, and style? This might be just the job for you.

Radio station programmers

Everyone is always nice to radio programmers. That's because they're the people who decide what gets played on the radio. They can make someone very rich at the flip of a switch.

Video directors

Video directing is one of the hottest jobs in music today. But it's not an easy job to get. Think you've got a great eye? Are you willing to put in the time? Are you a hard worker? This job is as cool as it gets.

Tour managers

Bands need lots of help when they go on the road. Tour managers cover all the bases. They organize schedules and decide who does what job. They stay in touch with the clubs, musicians, and record label. They wake up the band. And they put out the lights.

Superstars

This one's up to you!

Believe it or not, there are dozens of other careers in the music business. Any one of them could be yours. All you have to do is try. And remember three things the people in this book have said over and over again.

Believe in your passion.
Work hard.
Don't be afraid to ask for help.

So what are you waiting for? Get to work!

Glossary

alternative *(noun)* something you can choose instead of something else

article *(noun)* a piece of writing published in a newspaper or magazine

career *(noun)* jobs you have during your life

chord *(noun)* a combination of musical notes played at the same time

cliché *(noun)* an idea or phrase that's used so often that it no longer has very much meaning

client *(noun)* someone who uses the services of a professional person like a lawyer or accountant

composer *(noun)* someone who writes a piece of music

craft *(noun)* a skill or hobby that you have developed over time

digital *(adjective)* in a form that's usable by a computer

draft *(noun)* a version of something

editor *(noun)* the person in charge of all or part of a newspaper or magazine

effect *(noun)* in the music business, a sound that is created or shaped in an unusual way

ensnared *(adjective)* trapped

flexible *(adjective)* able to change

freelancer *(noun)* a worker who does not earn a salary but is paid for each job he or she does

gig *(noun)* a booking for a musician or a band to play

harmony *(noun)* a set of musical notes that are played or sung along with the melody

imply *(verb)* to suggest or mean something without saying it

improvise *(verb)* to make up something on the spot

inspire *(verb)* to influence

internship *(noun)* a job helping out at a place where you might want to work

interview *(noun)* a meeting at which someone is asked questions

label *(noun)* the name of a company (or a division within a company) that records and sells an artist's music

license *(verb)* in the music business, to sell someone the right to use a song

lyrics *(noun)* the words of a song

melody *(noun)* the tune of a song

mentor *(noun)* a person with wisdom and experience who can give you good personal and career advice

motivated *(adjective)* eager to do something

passion *(noun)* great love or enthusiasm

phrase *(noun)* a group of words

producer *(noun)* the person in charge of the entire process of making something

progression *(noun)* a series of musical tones or chords

rate *(noun)* a charge or a fee

royalty *(noun)* in the music business, money that gets paid to writers when their work is performed

sequence *(noun)* a collection of things (such as songs) that follow one another

spark *(verb)* to make something happen

studio *(noun)* a room or building in which an artist or musician works

technical *(adjective)* having to do with science or engineering

theme *(noun)* in the music business, the music at the beginning and end of a TV show

track *(noun)* a part of a recording. Songs are recorded in separate pieces called tracks. The final product is a combination of all the different tracks.

turntable *(noun)* a high-quality record player used by DJs

unique *(adjective)* one of a kind

vocabulary *(noun)* the words that a person uses and understands